AF577001

Perspectives of the Cross

C. NEIL STRAIT AND STAN TOLER

Beacon Hill Press of Kansas City
Kansas City, Missouri

Copyright 2002
by Beacon Hill Press of Kansas City

ISBN 083-411-948X

Printed in the
United States of America

Cover Design: Michael Walsh

All Scripture quotations are from the *Holy Bible, New International Version*® (NIV®). Copyright © 1973, 1978, 1984 by International Bible Society. Used by permission of Zondervan Publishing House. All rights reserved.

Library of Congress Control Number: 2001134039

10 9 8 7 6 5 4 3 2 1

Contents

JOEL 2:12-13

"Even now," declares the LORD,
"return to me with all your heart,
with fasting and weeping and mourning."
Rend your heart and not your garments.
Return to the LORD your God, for he
is gracious and compassionate, slow to
anger and abounding in love,
and he relents from sending calamity.

It is their darkest hours. They are homeless—hopeless. Tomorrow offers more of the same. Thus were the captive children of Israel—gripped by sadness and fear.

Their best days were behind them. Only memories of God's care and love haunted their hope. Imprisoned by their disobedience, they thought God had forsaken them.

Intruding upon their despair, the prophet Joel thundered, *Return to the LORD your God, for he is gracious and compassionate, slow to anger and abounding in love* (v. 13).

Where do you go when your heart is heavy and hurting . . . when life is at a dead end . . . when you've lost your joy? In this hopelessness there is a word from God. *Return to the LORD your God, for he is gracious and compassionate, slow to anger and abounding in love.*

In your despair there is God! He waits with gracious heart and merciful love to hear your cry and wipe your tears.

How do we find Him? *Return to me with all your heart, with fasting and weeping and mourning* (v. 12). It is a call to lay aside our sins and guilt, our disobedience, and turn with repentance and humility to God. This is the path of victory. He longs to welcome us into His grace and mercy and to restore our hope.

Joel's confirmation is encouraging—*Everyone who calls on the name of the LORD will be saved* (Joel 2:32).

PRAYER: *O God of love and mercy, I turn to You today with a repentant heart and with a will waiting to be summoned by Your call. Restore my soul, forgive my waywardness, and guide my life in paths of obedience. In Jesus' name I pray. Amen.*

THINK ON THIS: As we begin this Lenten season, may the depths of our souls be renewed through fasting, tears of confession, and obedience to God's will.

—C. Neil Strait

JOHN 1:14

The Word became flesh and made his dwelling among us. We have seen his glory, the glory of the One and Only, who came from the Father, full of grace and truth.

COL. 1:19-20

God was pleased to have all his fullness dwell in him, and through him to reconcile to himself all things.

The incarnation. The enfleshment of God. He *made his dwelling among us*. Who but God could have tolerated the sinful mess? Or the darkness . . . decay . . . despair? Who else would have known what to do?

But we need to know *why* He came. He came to redeem, to rescue, to splash hope into our despairing hearts. God did not need a big event or another miracle on His résumé. In obedience to the Father, Jesus came to show us the way to God.

How did He do it? He *came from the Father.* Paul puts it like this: *God was pleased to have all his fullness dwell in him* (Col. 1:19). Through His Son, God made himself vulnerable to rejection to confront human sin.

Yet in all this, Paul says that God was pleased with the plan. A God whose heart beats with love and grace is pleased to pour himself into human frame in order to become Savior.

It is a thought too deep to fathom and too high to attain. Faith and obedience are the only expressions that make sense.

PRAYER: *Eternal God, thank You for coming to me, to show yourself to me, and to be my Savior. Teach me how to walk in obedience and love. In Your Son's name I pray. Amen.*

THINK ON THIS: The incarnate Son of God, Jesus, shows us the Father by His life and love. We who claim Him as Savior are to show Him to the world.

—C. Neil Strait

Day 3

Matt. 4:1

Then Jesus was led by the Spirit into the desert to be tempted by the devil.

The 40-day duration of Lent is derived from the 40 days Jesus spent in the desert following His baptism. In Matthew 4 we read of His encounter with Satan.

Why was Jesus tempted? Did God need to see if His Son could withstand the test? Of course not—He was sinless. As we read in Heb. 4:15, *We do not have a high priest who is unable to sympathize with our weaknesses, but we have one who has been tempted in every way, just as we are—yet was without sin.* And God had already expressed divine approval of His Son at the Jordan.

I believe Jesus was tempted to expose Satan's tactics and to prove to us that we can have victory over him.

But the Church doesn't seem to know what to do with Satan these days. His name is still referred to in the Bible, of course, but often he has been written out of sermons and Sunday School lessons.

However, he seems to be making a comeback. Oklahoma City, Columbine High School, the terrorist attacks on the World Trade Center and the Pentagon—these have caused us to rethink the struggle between darkness and light. Could it be Satan? Of course! As Jesus said in John 10:10, *The thief comes only to steal and kill and destroy.*

Our Lord's experience in the desert prepared Him to be our sympathetic High Priest—as well as our source of victory. *Because he himself suffered when he was tempted, he is able to help those who are being tempted* (Heb. 2:18).

It's important for us to understand that Jesus faced this temptation as a man, not as the Son of God. How did He overcome? Through the same weapons that are available to us today—the Spirit (Matt. 4:1) and the Word (Matt. 4:4).

Jesus! what a Strength in weakness!
Let me hide myself in Him.
Tempted, tried, and sometimes failing,
He, my Strength, my vict'ry wins.

—J. Wilbur Chapman

PRAYER: *Lord, bring Your strength to my weakness. Shine Your light on the dark areas of my life. Help me to overcome the evil one through Your Spirit and through Your Word. In Jesus' name I pray. Amen.*

THINK ABOUT THIS: You are not tempted because you are evil; you are tempted because you are human.

—Stan Toler

Day 4

ISA. 61:1-3

The Spirit of the Sovereign LORD is on me,
because the LORD has anointed me to preach
good news to the poor. He has sent
me to bind up the brokenhearted,
to proclaim freedom for the captives
and release from darkness for the
prisoners, to proclaim the year of
the LORD's favor and the day of vengeance
of our God, to comfort all who mourn, and
provide for those who grieve in Zion—to
bestow on them a crown of beauty instead
of ashes, the oil of gladness instead of
mourning, and a garment of praise
instead of a spirit of despair.

"Creative" is a good word. "Creative" means having fine-tuned abilities to see what others cannot see. It is in the word family of "Creator." So it brings us eventually to God.

The God we worship is creative—doing what others cannot do, seeing what others cannot, being what others cannot be. It was this Creator God who invaded our sin-scarred world, bringing beauty out of ashes.

Harold Ivan Smith tells of a king who owned a beautiful diamond. But a problem developed—a scratch was detected in the middle of it. The king offered great riches and position for anyone who could remove the flaw. The best jewelers and artists came, but no one could remove the scratch.

One day a man appeared, optimistic about his chances of removing the blemish. He labored for weeks and finally presented the diamond to the king. To the king's astonishment, the flaw was still there—but the young man had carved a rose around it, using the scratch as a stem (Harold Ivan Smith, *A Decembered Grief* [Kansas City: Beacon Hill Press of Kansas City, 1999], 2-3).

Our creative God has come to bring beauty out of ashes. Where sin has marred relationships, Jesus mends them. Where sin has spawned despair, Jesus brings hope. Life can never be so etched with the residue of guilt and sin that Jesus, the creative Savior, cannot create a new life, a new beginning, and a new purpose.

Jesus has been *anointed . . . to preach good news . . . to bestow on them a crown of beauty instead of ashes* (Isa. 61:1, 3).

PRAYER: *Father, You designed and created a way out for me and have replaced my despair with hope through Your Son, Jesus. May I respond with obedience and love for this new life.*

THINK ON THIS: Life bears the scratches of sin deep in the human spirit. But God's redemptive power creates a new life out of the old and gives it a new purpose and joy.

—C. Neil Strait

LUKE 19:41

As he approached Jerusalem and saw the city, he wept over it.

Jesus wept while the crowd rejoiced. He wept because of the spiritual blindness of the people. He wept because of the sorry state of the religious community. He wept perhaps because He knew His hour of suffering had come.

Our Lord's last week, the events of what we call Holy Week, went like this:

SUNDAY: The Triumphal Entry into Jerusalem. *When he came near the place where the road goes down the Mount of Olives, the whole crowd of disciples began joyfully to praise God in loud voices for all the miracles they had seen: "Blessed is the King who comes in the name of the Lord!"* (Luke 19:37-38)

MONDAY: Jesus clears the Temple. *Then he entered the temple area and began driving out those who were selling. "It is written," he said to them, "My house will be a house of prayer"* (Luke 19:45-46).

TUESDAY: A day of questions. Jesus was drawn into a controversial exchange with the Jewish leaders. *They sent some of the Pharisees and Herodians to Jesus to catch him in his words* (Mark 12:13).

WEDNESDAY: Some say that it was the day Jesus was

anointed in Bethany. *While he was in Bethany . . . a woman came with an alabaster jar of very expensive perfume, made of pure nard. She broke the jar and poured the perfume on his head* (Mark 14:3).

THURSDAY: Jesus spent a last night with His disciples preparing for Passover. It was also the night Jesus washed the feet of His disciples, the evening of the Last Supper (John 13).

FRIDAY: Good Friday. The trial and crucifixion (Mark 15).

SATURDAY: Jesus awaits the Resurrection.

PRAYER: *In my busy week, O Lord, help me not forget the awesome events that brought lasting hope to my life. Thank You that when Your hour came, You did not turn away. In Your name I pray. Amen.*

THINK ABOUT THIS: Jesus came to save the lost, the last, and the least.

—Stan Toler

Day 6

Matt. 21:9

Hosanna to the Son of David!
Blessed is he who comes in the name of the Lord!
Hosanna in the highest!

The population of Jerusalem had more than tripled in celebration of Passover, the observance commemorating Israel's deliverance from Egypt. As many as 2 million people may have swarmed the Holy City. The Roman military was alert to the threat of assassinations, riots, and arguments with such a crowd present.

Into this setting Jesus made His triumphal entry. It was the only time in His ministry that Jesus actually allowed any sort of public demonstration on His behalf. Why now? Partly to fulfill prophecy, as recorded in Zech. 9:9—*Rejoice greatly, O Daughter of Zion! Shout, Daughter of Jerusalem! See, your king comes to you, righteous and having salvation, gentle and riding on a donkey.*

He could have permitted it to force the Jewish leaders to take some course of action. They had hoped to arrest Jesus after Passover, but God ordained that His Son would be seized during Passover. When they saw the response of the people, they had to do something.

As Jesus rode through the city streets on the donkey, the crowd rejoiced. Some laid their cloaks on the road. Others cut branches from the trees and spread them on the road, shouting, "Hosanna!" which means "Save now!"

But the triumph soon turned to tragedy. Those who sought to make Him king cursed Him. The Galilean was paraded shamefully down the same road of His royal entrance.

Let us link our hearts with the rejoicing crowd. We can use this Lenten season to voice our honest praise, to show Him how much we love Him by the dedication of our lives to His service.

PRAYER: *Father, give me grace to know more fully the Christ who was humbled and exalted. Give me a new song of praise for the One who comes in Your name. In Jesus' name I pray. Amen.*

THINK ABOUT THIS: Jesus rode a humble donkey and was lifted to a borrowed cross—but God raised Him from the dead and exalted His name above every other name!

—Stan Toler

Day 7

JOHN 11:57

The chief priests and Pharisees had given orders that if anyone found out where Jesus was, he should report it so that they might arrest him.

John 11:46-57 tells about the plot to kill Jesus. Three short years of ministry, miracles, and love have come to this. He, who embodied love and compassion, is met with cruel hatred.

It's a tragic reminder of evil forces in the world. Sin has no boundaries. Evil hits with shocking frequency. Sin respects no one. There is no exempt list.

Sin impacts life in every area—spiritually, physically, mentally, socially—*every* area. Yet it's seldom recognized or talked about. The word "sin" has been dropped from the vocabulary in a blame-others age. The title of Karl Menninger's book says it all: *Whatever Became of Sin?*

The fact is that sin and evil are as alive today as when they inflicted their ugly venom on Jesus. If anything, it has taken on uglier hues and more vicious forms—Oklahoma City, Columbine High School, the World Trade Center, the Pentagon. But we're not surprised. Sin and evil have at their very center the ingredients for destruction—selfishness, disrespect, and disobedience. One would wonder why anyone would harbor such potential dynamite for sorrow and conflict.

But there's another option—the way of Jesus. Those who follow Him know forgiveness, love, hope, and purpose. They allow Him to change them with His matchless love and grace.

Lent gives us time to assess our lives. Where does sin enter? Do we harbor it, giving it room to grow and wreak havoc? These are difficult questions we must answer.

PRAYER: *Father, allow no mediocre commitment to You in my life, tolerate no halfhearted devotion to Your way. Through my obedience, Lord, forbid sin to establish any beachhead in my soul. In Jesus' name I pray. Amen.*

THINK ON THIS: Sin is crafty and creative. It does not barge into our hearts, but by subtle ways it is content to inch into our minds and spirits. Our caution must be careful and prayerful.

—C. Neil Strait

JOHN 12:23-25

The hour has come for the Son of Man to be glorified. I tell you the truth, unless a kernel of wheat falls to the ground and dies, it remains only a single seed. But if it dies, it produces many seeds. The man who loves his life will lose it, while the man who hates his life in this world will keep it for eternal life.

The seed is a beautiful metaphor Jesus used to illustrate a great spiritual truth: there can be no life without death. Now, I'm no "green thumb." I've put more plants on death row than any other weekend horticulturist in the world. But I think I understand the principle of the seed.

It's a thing of wonder to watch a farmer plant a seed that appears weak and insignificant. But when it's planted, is buried in the dark ground, and dies, it becomes a miracle of life and abundance. Spiritually, like a seed, we're weak and insignificant. But when we die, a miracle of life and abundance begins to take place.

The problem is—we don't want to die! Physically, we're born with a will to survive. But spiritually, our "will to live" presents us with quite a dilemma.

In John 12 Jesus faced the same dilemma. He faced not only physical death but also total submission to His Father's will: death to atone for the sins of the world. Later, in verse 27, He said, *Now my heart is troubled, and what shall I say? "Father, save me from this hour"? No, it was for this very reason I came to this hour.*

Abundant life is the result of His sacrifice to accomplish the Father's will.

Do you want your life to be productive? Then die to self! And live to God!

If we died with Christ, we believe that we will also live with him. For we know that since Christ was raised from the dead, he cannot die again; death no longer has mastery over him. The death he died, he died to sin once for all; but the life he lives, he lives to God. In the same way, count yourselves dead to sin but alive to God in Christ Jesus (Rom. 6:8-11).

PRAYER: *Lord, I want my life to be productive and fruitful. Help me to stop surviving and start thriving—living life to its fullest in You. In Your name I pray. Amen.*

THINK ABOUT THIS: The best way to live *in* the world is to live *above* it.

—Stan Toler

LUKE 22:52-54

Then Jesus said to the chief priests, the officers of the temple guard, and the elders, who had come for him, "Am I leading a rebellion, that you have come with swords and clubs? Every day I was with you in the temple courts, and you did not lay a hand on me. But this is your hour—when darkness reigns." Then seizing him, they led him away and took him into the house of the high priest.

God arrested? Yes, arrogant religious folk threw the Creator in jail! After Jesus and His disciples had left the Upper Room, they headed to the Garden of Gethsemane, on the Mount of Olives. Earlier in Luke 22, verse 39, we read, *Jesus went out as usual to the Mount of Olives*. "As usual" means there was a pattern. Jesus had a routine—a regular devotional time—and Judas the betrayer knew it. That's when he led the Roman soldiers and Temple guards to the garden, where they could arrest Jesus.

There Jesus had prayed, *Father, if you are willing, take this cup from me; yet not my will, but yours be done* (Luke 22:42). What did the "cup" represent? Every sin, every abuse, every humiliation, every suffering known to man. It was an agonizing moment for our Lord. Verse 44 says, *And being in anguish, he prayed more earnestly, and his sweat was like drops of blood falling to the ground.*

Then came the kiss of betrayal. In Bible times a kiss

was a customary greeting, much like a handshake. It was a sign of affection and respect. But not on this night. This night it was a symbol of betrayal.

Enraged by the awful injustice, one of the disciples, Peter, pulled out his sword and tried to make two soldiers out of one. Jesus rebuked him, and then, without any resistance, the God of the universe gave himself over to the arresting officers.

PRAYER: *Thank you, Lord, for turning yourself in for me. Teach me how to submit my will to the Father's will. Help me not to be sleeping when I should be praying, talking when I should be listening, or fighting when I should be submitting. In Your name I pray. Amen.*

THINK ABOUT THIS: Decide today whether you're going to go through life pretending like Judas, fighting like Peter, or submitting like Jesus.

—Stan Toler

Day 10

John 18:25

As Simon Peter stood warming himself, he was asked, "You are not one of his disciples, are you?" He denied it, saying, "I am not."

Peter was known as "the Rock." It was a name Jesus had given to him when Peter's brother, Andrew, introduced him. By his allegiance to the Master, Peter lived up to his name. Some followers couldn't accept the teachings of Jesus. *This is a hard teaching. Who can accept it?* they said (John 6:60). Many deserted Him. But Jesus asked the remaining disciples point blank, *You do not want to leave too, do you?* Peter, "the Rock," answered quickly, *Lord, to whom shall we go? You have the words of eternal life. We believe and know that you are the Holy One of God* (John 6:68-69).

The last time Jesus and the Twelve were together, He told them that He would be leaving and that where He was going they could not go. Peter asked, *Lord, why can't I follow you now? I will lay down my life for you.* Jesus replied, *Will you really lay down your life for me? I tell you the truth, before the rooster crows, you will disown me three times!* (John 13:37-38)

Within a matter of hours, "the Rock" crumbled, just as Jesus said he would. Can you imagine how those little hairs on the back of the disciple's neck must have stood at attention when that old rooster began to crow?

What was the difference between Peter's actions and those of Judas? The difference was that Peter not only expressed remorse for his sins—he repented from them. Jesus gave him a second chance. That's love!

Love so amazing, so divine,
Demands my soul, my life, my all!

—Isaac Watts

PRAYER: *Jesus, Your love is amazing! Thank You that You give the hard cases a second chance. Please don't ever give up on me. In Your name I pray. Amen.*

THINK ABOUT THIS: When you surround yourself with wrongdoers, doing wrong becomes quite easy.

—Stan Toler

Day 11

JOHN 18:28-29

Then the Jews led Jesus from Caiaphas to the palace of the Roman governor. By now it was early morning, and to avoid ceremonial uncleanness the Jews did not enter the palace; they wanted to be able to eat the Passover. So Pilate came out to them and asked, "What charges are you bringing against this man?"

Though they had neither the right nor the authority to kill Jesus without Pilate's approval, the Jewish council determined to do just that. Jews did not like Pontius Pilate, but nonetheless they had to work the system to get what they wanted.

Pilate didn't see Jesus as a threat to Rome and told the Jews, *I find no basis for a charge against him* (John 18:38). He tried everything he could to avoid a Jewish court case, especially at Passover. He even attempted to pawn Jesus off on Herod, but Herod returned Him to Pilate.

Next, Pilate tried to bargain with the Jewish leaders. It was customary at Passover for the governor to release a prisoner. Why not Jesus? The option was to offer a prisoner named Barabbas, a thief and murderer. Who would want a man like that back on the streets? But the chief priests and elders persuaded the people to demand that Barabbas be released.

Pilate still was hard pressed to find a reason to crucify Jesus. Hoping to appease the crowd, he had Him flogged.

The soldiers twisted together a crown of thorns and put it on his head. They clothed him in a purple robe and went up to him again and again, saying, "Hail, king of the Jews!" And they struck him in the face (John 19:2-3).

Surely this display would satisfy the crowd. But Pilate had failed again.

Finally he gave in to the crowd's demands and handed the guiltless Jesus over to be crucified. From a human viewpoint, the trial of Jesus was the greatest miscarriage of justice in history. But from the divine viewpoint, it was the greatest fulfillment of prophecy and the greatest unfolding of salvation's plan.

PRAYER: *Jesus, my heart is broken when I read in the Gospel accounts of how You were so unfairly treated. Help me to learn how to be just and fair with others. In Your name I pray. Amen.*

THINK ABOUT THIS: The Cross is where humanity did its worst and God did His best.

—Stan Toler

Day 12

JOHN 19:16-18

Finally Pilate handed him over to them to be crucified. So the soldiers took charge of Jesus. Carrying his own cross, he went out to the place of the skull (which in Aramaic is called Golgotha). Here they crucified him, and with him two others—one on each side and Jesus in the middle.

Jesus was nailed to a cross next to criminals who had broken the law and were caught. But what had Jesus done? Pilate couldn't answer that question, nor could others who bore responsibility.

Were they uninformed? Obviously. Doubtful? Certainly. Cowards? Absolutely. Politically minded? To be sure. But would not some sense prevail when you're handling the Son of God? No sensible answer will ever come. Great minds have searched for motives and answers, only to be left wanting. There are none.

Jesus was nailed to a cross—and they thought it was finished. Whatever reasons they thought they had, whatever problems they thought He might cause, nothing was finished by nailing Jesus to a cross. Sin doesn't stay hidden for long. Crucifying Jesus did not finish Jesus. When they laid Him in a tomb, they thought it was over. They thought He was history. Finished. Done.

But it had just begun! Through the Crucifixion and

Resurrection, God triumphed over His enemies—death, hell, and the grave. The Resurrection settled the question of who was in charge. They thought they had gotten rid of Jesus but soon realized their problems had only begun.

What they had not reckoned with was that this was God whom they had nailed to a tree.

Be careful what you do with Jesus. Remember: He is God's Son, with His Father's authority and power. With His love, grace, and mercy, He waits to invade and capture every heart.

PRAYER: *Eternal God, may I see You in all You do in the life of Your Son, and may I be drawn to Him and, in so doing, be drawn to You. In His name I pray. Amen.*

THINK ON THIS: They nailed Jesus to a cross for no reason. God was in Christ, at the Cross, reconciling the world for a reason.

—C. Neil Strait

Day 13

JOHN 19:16-18

Finally Pilate handed him over to them to be crucified. So the soldiers took charge of Jesus. Carrying his own cross, he went out to the place of the skull (which in Aramaic is called Golgotha). Here they crucified him him, and with him two others—one on each side and Jesus in the middle.

A picture of the Crucifixion with a large figure behind the portrait of Christ is displayed in an Italian church. The nail that pierces the hand of Jesus goes through to the hand of God. The spear thrust into the side of Jesus goes through to the side of God (Erwin W. Lutzer, *Ten Lies About God* [Nashville: Word Publishing, 2000], 72).

The artist depicts the pain and sorrow the Father felt when His Son was dying on the Cross. Bishop Stephen Neill wrote, "If the crucifixion of Jesus . . . is in some way, as Christians have believed, the dying of God himself, then . . . we can understand what God is like" (Quoted in Lutzer, *Ten Lies About God,* 72).

Calvary was not the work of a person. The plan and the price were God's doing. You and I must see God at the center of Calvary, or it becomes simply a human event, subject to ridicule and debate. But it is God, at Calvary, giving His Son, feeling the pain and rejection of human torture. And He does it for you and me.

The Cross is a picture of God. His coming to give His

only Son for our sins is all we need to know about God—now. What it tells us about God overwhelms us. We are humbled by His love. What we know, then, invites us to believe in Him and to entrust our lives to Him.

When we see what God is like it gives new meaning to Good Friday. God is suffering with His Son; God feels the pain. It is God who is nailed to the Cross.

Jesus is God's representative to bring us back to God. It is the great thought of Calvary.

PRAYER: *O Lord, I am debtor to You for taking my place at Calvary. May my life reflect gratitude through my love for You and my obedience to Your will. In Your name I pray. Amen.*

THINK ON THIS: God paid the heavy price of Calvary so that sinners might be set free to live life more abundantly.

—C. Neil Strait

Day 14

Isa. 53:5-6

He was pierced for our transgressions,
he was crushed for our iniquities;
the punishment that brought us peace was upon him,
and by his wounds we are healed.
We all, like sheep, have gone astray,
each of us has turned to his own way;
and the Lord has laid on him the iniquity of us all.

Mozart has a wonderful line in one of his compositions: "Help me to remember that I was the cause of your journey" (Quoted in Lutzer, *Ten Lies About God*, 180).

As we walk through Lent, it's good to remember that Christ is on the Cross on our behalf. Our sins are the reason for Calvary. Paul reminds us that *all have sinned and fall short of the glory of God* (Rom. 3:23). It's sobering to know we had a part in our Lord's journey to death.

It causes us to reflect on the journey, to review its reason, even to feel the sorrow and know that we are there.

Such reflection leads to repentance. We see the Cross in a deeper dimension. We feel its pain and price in a new way. Out of godly sorrow comes repentance, which is what God planned at Calvary. He planned our redemption by the death of His Son.

His journey was because of us and for us! God's purpose was to bring life out of sin's death, to bring hope out of despair. To miss this is to miss the purpose of the journey.

Therefore, Lent is not just a time for reflection. It is a time for resolution, decision, and commitment. Such determination calls for the heart to be engaged—to be witness to His love and to be involved in His purpose. Then Calvary's purpose will have been fulfilled.

This Lenten season may we say to Jesus, *Help me to remember that I was the cause of Your journey.*

PRAYER: *Father, as I journey through these Lenten days, help me remember that I was the cause of Your journey. In Christ's name I pray. Amen.*

THINK ON THIS: Yes, I was the cause of Christ's journey. But the question is, will I be part of His kingdom now?

—C. Neil Strait

Day 15

ISA. 53:5

By his wounds we are healed.

The Prince of Wales visited 36 severely wounded men after a war just to shake their hands and express his thanks.

When he had finished his visits, he noted that he had counted only 35 and inquired about the one remaining. He was told that the man was so severely wounded, and his appearance so distorted, that a visit would be unbearable for the prince.

He insisted and was ushered into the room. As he stood by the bed, he stooped and kissed the soldier. The prince was heard to say in broken voice, "Wounded for me!"

We cannot read the story of Calvary, its crucifixion, its torture, and rejection without realizing that all of it was for us. The Lenten period brings the Calvary story home to us. We feel the pain, the rejection, the sorrow. We know, then, what great price Jesus paid for our redemption. He was wounded for us. Tricia McCary Rhodes in her book *Contemplating the Cross* writes, "Until we're willing to confront the terrible trauma of Gethsemane, the Cross will exist as a symbol of our religion instead of the very heartbeat of our faith" ([Minneapolis: Bethany House, 1998], 18).

Rhodes puts more of her thoughts about the Cross in these words:

Man of sorrows . . . You have looked sorrow in the face and wept in its wasteland. And though you grieved to the point of death, you did not die. Not then, O God, in the soil of your sadness, seeds of hope are planted for a dying world. Let me search deeply this moment of yours. Open wide my eyes that I might glimpse your eternal sacrifice. Take me into your dark night, and we will acquaint ourselves together with the paradox of grief's glory (Rhodes, *Contemplating the Cross,* 25).

When we have had such a visit, our response can be only "He was wounded for me!"

PRAYER: *O God, my Father, You were wounded for me. For Your gift of life and love, I am eternally grateful. I pray in Your name. Amen.*

THINK ON THIS: We can bring no gift nor do any great deed that would in any way repay our Savior for what He has done for us. We are eternal debtors.

—C. Neil Strait

Day 16

Rom. 5:6-8

At just the right time, when we were still powerless, Christ died for the ungodly. Very rarely will anyone die for a righteous man, though for a good man someone might possibly dare to die. But God demonstrates his own love for us in this: While we were still sinners, Christ died for us.

These words are hope for all who have failed, challenge for all who have labored under the guilt of past sins: *God demonstrates his own love for us in this: While we were still sinners, Christ died for us* (Rom. 5:8).

A famous man died in the prime of his life, and a newspaper reporter interviewed his mother. Among his first questions was "We'd like to know at what stage of his life you loved him the most. . . . Was it when he was a public personality, an author, a celebrity, a teenager, or an adult?"

The mother thought for a few moments and then answered, "You know, it happened one afternoon when my son was seven. He knew he had hurt me by something he did. As I was reading the paper, my young son rushed into the room. He fell on his knees and buried his face in my lap. As he sobbed, he said, 'Mommy, please forgive me—I'm sorry I hurt you!'" She said he was heartbroken. "When I think of when I loved him most, it was then."

The reporter was startled by the answer and replied, "That seems like such an insignificant happening. Why does that stand out in your mind?"

The mother's reply: "I think it was because he needed me to love him so much at that moment" (H. B. London Jr. and Neil B. Wiseman, *They Call Me Pastor* [Ventura, Calif.: Regal Books, 2000], 83).

Just when we need His love, at our worst moment, when life seems a total wreck, you find love in Jesus—now! When we need something or someone to fill the void and lift life to a higher level, we find it in Jesus. It's the great message that rings from the Cross.

PRAYER: *Eternal God, You loved me when I was unlovable, when I was a sinner, when I was helpless. Thank You for love that not only lifts me but keeps me in Your care. In Jesus' name I pray. Amen.*

THINK ON THIS: Every life comes to a moment of needing love, understanding, hope, and forgiveness. Jesus majors in all of these. And the kind He gives cannot be found anywhere else.

—C. Neil Strait

Day 17

LUKE 23:33-34

When they came to the place called the Skull, there they crucified him, along with the criminals—one on his right, the other on his left. Jesus said, "Father, forgive them, for they do not know what they are doing."

Our Lord's last seven words from the Cross are significant. As Jesus hung there, dying for the sins of the world, He prayed, *Father, forgive them.*

Jesus had been betrayed and denied by His disciples.

He had been beaten, mocked, spat upon.

He had been publicly humiliated.

Nails had been driven through His hands and feet, and His side had been pierced.

But instead of curses, blasphemy, or words of wrath, people on that day heard, *Father, forgive them.*

It would have been a lot easier for Jesus to pray, "Go get them, Father!" "Take them out!" He could have called 10,000 angels to set Him free, but He didn't.

Instead, He simply prayed that God would be gracious to those who were trying to destroy Him. That is a difficult prayer to pray. But Jesus always practiced what He preached. You'll remember that in the Sermon on the Mount (Matt. 6:15) He said, *If you do not forgive men their sins, your Father will not forgive your sins.*

I find it remarkable that not only did Jesus pray for their forgiveness—He even argued on their behalf: *For they do not know what they are doing*. It's as if He was saying, "Here's why You should forgive them, Father: They were ignorant of their own sin."

Sin does that to us. It blinds us. It confuses us. Thank God for His patience and lovingkindness. And thank God we're living in a day of grace and not judgment. Jesus died to reconcile lost sinners to God.

There are all kinds of prayers. There are bedtime prayers, mealtime prayers, desperate prayers (like those tossed to the heavens in the last seconds of a basketball game). But the highest level of prayer may be intercessory—praying for the needs of others. When Jesus prayed, *Father, forgive them,* for whom was He praying? Pilate, the soldiers, the angry mob, His disciples who had betrayed and denied Him?

Or was He praying for you and me?

PRAYER: *Thank You, Lord, not only for being so forgiving, but also for showing me how to be forgiving. Help me to be forgiving. Help me to be a better intercessor. In Your name I pray. Amen.*

THINK ABOUT THIS: 1 cross + 3 nails = 4 given

—Stan Toler

Day 18

LUKE 23:43

I tell you the truth, today you will be with me in paradise.

The second word from the Cross was an answered prayer. The criminal at the side of the innocent Savior prayed, *Jesus, remember me when you come into your kingdom* (Luke 23:42). Jesus responded, *Today you will be with me in paradise.*

There were three crosses on Golgatha's hill. A man dying *in* sin hung on one of the crosses. On another hung a man dying *from* sin. On the middle cross hung the Son of God, who was dying *for* sin. An insulting, cursing crowd gathered nearby. Unbelievably, one of the criminals hanging there joined with the crowd and mocked Jesus: *Aren't you the Christ? Save yourself and us!* (v. 39).

Some scholars say that it was a common practice for the soldiers to gag with a cloth those whom they were crucifying. It seemed their intent was to keep the condemned from returning insults. But for some reason neither Jesus nor the two criminals were gagged that day. Perhaps the soldiers were curious. Perhaps even these rough soldiers wanted to hear every word the Prince of Peace would say.

Verses 40-44 of Luke 23 records, *But the other criminal rebuked him, "Don't you fear God . . . since you are under the same sentence? We are punished justly, for we are getting what our deeds deserve. But this man has done nothing wrong."* Then he simply asked Jesus to remember him. One was praying to be set free from the *consequences* of his sin, the other praying to be set free from his *sin*.

Jesus kept His promise *Whoever comes to me I will never drive away* (John 6:37). Jesus did not refuse the criminal's plea for mercy. He did not say, "First, you'll have to join the church, be baptized, and put into the offering plate 10 percent of everything you earn. That would have been impossible. At that moment, there was nothing he could do to gain Paradise except to rely on the grace of Christ. Was he an exception? Yes! But, then again, so are we. None of us deserves the grace of our Lord. Who among us really deserves Paradise?

The dying thief rejoiced to see
That fountain in his day;
And there may I, tho' vile as he,
Wash all my sins away.

—William Cowper

PRAYER: *Lord Jesus, thank You for the promise of Paradise. I want to see it! Most of all, I want to see You! In Your name I pray. Amen.*

THINK ABOUT THIS: If we could merit our own salvation, Jesus would never have died to provide it.

—Stan Toler

MATT. 27:45-46

From the sixth hour until the ninth hour
darkness came over all the land.
About the ninth hour Jesus cried out
in a loud voice . . . My God, my God,
why have you forsaken me?

After our Lord spoke His second word on the Cross, darkness came—universal darkness. For three long hours the earth was covered with a blanket of gloom. The sun refused to shine because "the Light of the world" had taken upon himself the gloomy despair of our sins. Isaac Watts wrote,

Well might the sun in darkness hide,
And shut His glories in
When Christ, the mighty Maker, died
For man, the creature's, sin.

There was an awful loneliness in His words. He had been forsaken by His closest followers. Now He felt forsaken by God, His Father.

Until this moment He had enjoyed the uninterrupted presence of His Heavenly Father. At His baptism God was there—even giving the worthy endorsement *This is my Son, whom I love; with him I am well pleased* (Matt. 3:17).

When Jesus was led into the desert to be tempted by the devil, His Father was there. The angels of heaven even came and attended to Him.

When Jesus agonized in the Garden of Gethsemene, His Father was there.

When Jesus was taken before Pilate, His Father was there.

When the soldiers beat and mocked Jesus, His Father was there.

Even during the painful moment when they drove the nails through His hands and feet, the Father was there.

But at that incredible moment when Jesus took our sins upon himself, He was alone. God the Father had turned His head.

If the Father turned from His own Son as He bore the sins of the world, how unsightly must its sin be to Him today! Jesus, who had never sinned, bore *our* sin as well as its accompanying separation from God. 2 Cor. 5:21 puts it this way: *God made him who had no sin to be sin for us, so that in him we might become the righteousness of God.*

PRAYER: *Jesus, I can't imagine the physical or emotional pain You endured on the Cross for me. Thank You for overcoming such loneliness so that I might have fellowship with the Father. In Your precious name I pray. Amen.*

THINK ABOUT THIS: Jesus was forsaken by the Father so that *we* would *never* be forsaken.

—Stan Toler

Day 20

John 19:28

Later, knowing that all was now completed,
and so that the Scripture would be fulfilled,
Jesus said, "I am thirsty."

Jesus had been silent for some time. Those who were near the Cross probably wondered if He would ever speak again. His body was feverish from the lacerations on His back and the open wounds on His hands and feet. He had lost a tremendous amount of blood. Yet He found strength to say, *I am thirsty.*

How tormenting His thirst must have been! Humans can go without food for many hours, days, even weeks. But the body can't survive long without water. Jesus' need for water reveals His humanity. Though some theologians today question our Lord's *deity,* many in the Early Church questioned His *humanity*.

Christ came into the world as a baby. He grew up as a child under the watchful eye of His earthly guardians. Luke says in his Gospel, *Jesus grew in wisdom and stature, and in favor with God and men* (Luke 2:52). Fully God, yet fully man. He hungered and ate. He thirsted and drank. He tired and rested.

He wept.

He suffered.

He died.

Real life, human experiences. What a paradox that

Jesus, the Creator of every lake, every river, and every mountain spring would say, *I am thirsty*!

There's also a glimpse of deity in those words. Over 100 prophecies in the Old Testament concern the crucifixion of Christ. Why did Jesus say, *I am thirsty*? John says, *So that Scripture would be fulfilled*. What scripture? Ps. 69:3, a picture of the Savior.

Jesus once told a story about a rich man who died and found himself in hell. He was thirsty and begged Lazarus to dip the tip of his finger in water and cool his tongue. When Jesus died on the Cross, He entered the gates of hell, a place of eternal thirst. At the Feast of Tabernacles Jesus said, *If anyone is thirsty, let him come to me and drink. Whoever believes in me, as the Scripture has said, streams of living water will flow from within him* (John 7:37-38).

PRAYER: *Jesus, today I thirst. I thirst for You. I thirst for righteousness. Please fill me. I ask this in Your name. Amen.*

THINK ABOUT THIS: He who was the water of life was condemned to thirst.

—Stan Toler

Day 21

JOHN 19:26-27

When Jesus saw his mother there, and the disciple whom he loved standing nearby, he said to his mother, "Dear woman, here is your son," and to the disciple, "Here is your mother." From that time on, this disciple took her into his home.

What must it have been like for Mary, the mother of Jesus, to watch her son die? No mother ever dreams of outliving her children, let alone watching them die such a torturous death. How do you suppose Mary felt that day? What did she think about?

Maybe her mind raced back to the angel's announcement: *Greetings, you who are highly favored! The Lord is with you. . . . Do not be afraid, Mary, you have found favor with God. You will be with child and give birth to a son, and you are to give him the name Jesus. He will be great and will be called the Son of the Most High. The Lord God will give him the throne of his father David, and he will reign over the house of Jacob forever; his kingdom will never end* (Luke 1:28, 30-33).

Mary's dreams for her son were exceeded only by God's. But where's the greatness now? The crowd despises Him. Where's the throne? He hangs on a cross. Where's the kingdom? Even His disciples are gone.

Mary had prepared herself for His birth, but not for His death. When He said, *I thirst*, you can be sure that she would have raced to get her son a cup of water, just as she had done a hundred times before. Now she longed just to hold Him in her arms and whisper, "It's all right, Son. Everything is going to be all right." Even though she knew it wasn't all right.

Since Joseph had passed away, Jesus, being the oldest, had provided for His mother. Who would care for her now? He looks to John the disciple and says, *Here is your mother.* In other words, "You must take My place now." Scripture tells us that from that day on John cared for Mary.

Jesus is looking to you today. He's saying, "You must take My place." You are His hands and feet in this world. After the Resurrection He commissioned all His followers, *As the Father has sent me, I am sending you* (John 20:21).

PRAYER: *Today, Lord, I have a greater appreciation for the things You said from the Cross. Like John, I make myself available to do Your work. In Your name I pray. Amen.*

THINK ABOUT THIS: Mary lost a son that day, but the world gained a Savior.

—Stan Toler

Day 22

John 12:32

But I, when I am lifted up from the earth,
will draw all men to myself.

The debate continues over lethal injection as a means of capital punishment. The discussions are usually focused on what's "humane" and what's not. Yet there's a noticeable absence of debate concerning the cruelty of crucifixion. Spikes were driven through the hands and feet as the condemned was nailed to a cross timber. Death was often a welcomed relief to the crucified.

One of our most loved hymns says:

On a hill far away stood an old rugged cross,
The emblem of suff'ring and shame;
And I love that old cross, where the dearest and best
For a world of lost sinners was slain.

—George Bennard

Why do we love an emblem of suffering and shame? The apostle Paul wrote, *May I never boast except in the cross of our Lord Jesus Christ* (Gal. 6:14). What did he mean? In order for it to make any sense, we have to look beyond the Cross to see the empty tomb. We must see the total plan of God's redemption. The agony of the Cross was a prelude to the victory of the empty tomb.

The apostle Paul saw the fulfillment of prophecy, the completion of the plan. He boasted in the glory of the Cross. He saw Jesus *lifted up from the earth*. Without the Cross, without His suffering and death, there could be no salvation.

Without the shedding of blood there is no forgiveness (Heb. 9:22).

PRAYER: *Lord, I cherish the old rugged Cross. Thank You for transforming a symbol of suffering and shame into a symbol of life and hope. In Your name I pray. Amen.*

THINK ABOUT THIS: Had Christ been put to death in our day, what symbol would be prominently displayed on our church steeples?

—Stan Toler

Day 23

LUKE 23:44-46

It was now about the sixth hour, and darkness came over the whole land until the ninth hour, for the sun stopped shining. And the curtain of the temple was torn in two. Jesus called out with a loud voice, "Father, into your hands I commit my spirit." When he had said this, he breathed his last.

His first words on the Cross were a prayer: *Father, forgive them.* Appropriately, so were His last words: *Father, into your hands I commit my spirit.* Both revealed the depth of love and trust the Father and Son communicated to each other.

Many times I have stood at gravesides and committed the bodies of my brothers and sisters in faith to the ground, "earth to earth, ashes to ashes, dust to dust," as they await resurrection. Since it is appointed that all of us will die, our spirits are committed to an eternal destination.

But our destination will be determined by what we commit ourselves to today. Paul wrote in Rom. 12:1, *I urge you, brothers, in view of God's mercy, to offer your bodies as living sacrifices, holy and pleasing to God.*

The problem with living sacrifices is that they keep crawling off the altar. The key to holy living is death—spiritual death to self and selfishness.

Jesus really did die. The Roman officials made certain of it. John records, *The soldiers therefore came and broke the legs of the first man who had been crucified with Jesus, and then those of the other. But when they came to Jesus and found that he was already dead, they did not break his legs. Instead, one of the soldiers pierced Jesus' side with a spear, bringing a sudden flow of blood and water* (John 19:32-34).

Has there been a spiritual death to sin and the flesh? Have you committed your spirit to the Father? Is your all on the altar? Have you made a complete sacrifice?

Is your all on the altar of sacrifice laid?
Your heart does the Spirit control?
You can only be blest
And have peace and sweet rest
As you yield Him your body and soul.

—Elisha A. Hoffman

PRAYER: *Father, into Your hands I commit all that I am or ever hope to be. Take me and lead me in the way everlasting. In Your Son's name I pray. Amen.*

THINK ABOUT THIS: When we commit everything into the hands of God, then everything is left up to Him.

—Stan Toler

Day 24

JOHN 19:30

Jesus said, "It is finished." With that,
he bowed his head and gave up his spirit.

Ebenezer Wooten, an old-fashioned backwoods evangelist, held tent revivals. One Monday morning, as he was pulling up his stakes and folding his tent before moving on to the next town, a man confronted him, asking, "Preacher, what do I have to do to get saved?"

The old evangelist said, "'fraid you're too late. Ain't nothin' you can do. Jesus done it all when He said, 'It is finished'!"

When Jesus said, *It is finished,* He meant that the ultimate penalty for sin had been paid in full. Notice that He didn't say, "*I* am finished." He said, "*It* is finished" (emphasis added). In the Greek this means, "It is finished, it stands finished, and it always will be finished."

This is a word of accomplishment. Jesus was always on a mission. At the tender age of 12, He had an urgency about doing His Father's business. As He matured and began public ministry, His sense of urgency never abated. *As long as it is day, we must do the work of him who sent me. Night is coming, when no one can work* (John 9:4). Therefore, when Jesus came to the consummation of His mission, He triumphantly declared, "It is finished."

But we must note that His enemies didn't "finish Him

off." He gave up His life. Had His life been *taken*, Jesus would have been a victim. But since He *gave up His life*, He was a victor. He said, *The reason my Father loves me is that I lay down my life—only to take it up again. No one takes it from me, but I lay it down of my own accord. I have authority to lay it down and authority to take it up again* (John 10:17-18).

Philip P. Bliss wrote these stirring words:

Lifted up was He to die;
"It is finished," was His cry.
Now in heav'n exalted high—
Hallelujah! what a Savior!

Is Jesus your Savior? He wants to be. All you have to do is call on His name. The Scripture says, *Everyone who calls on the name of the Lord will be saved* (Rom. 10:13).

PRAYER: *Thank You, Lord, that You did not quit until Your mission was completed. Give me the endurance to complete the mission You've given to me. In Your name I pray. Amen.*

THINK ABOUT THIS: The cross-less life is a crown-less death.

—Stan Toler

Day 25

1 Pet. 3:18

Christ died for sins once for all,
the righteous for the unrighteous,
to bring you to God.

Let me take you to a hill called Mount Calvary, the place where Jesus Christ died. History is forever marked by what occurred there—the place of the Cross. Some refer to it as Golgotha, or simply "the place of the skull." It is a hill located just outside Jerusalem that contains cliffside impressions resembling a skull.

According to biblical law, sin offerings had to be made "outside the camp." Many offerings took place at the altar in the Tabernacle, but sin offerings were made outside the walls of the city. Heb. 13:12 says, *Jesus also suffered outside the city gate to make the people holy through his own blood.*

It was a place of death for common criminals. But for the sinless Son of God, it was the place of the sin offering.

The cross was a slow, agonizing, humiliating form of capital punishment reserved for criminals or political rebels.

Had Jesus been one of the criminals or insurrectionists, we would not have remembered that day in history. But He was nothing of the sort. The Man on the middle cross was the very Son of God, the Lamb of God who came to take away the sins of the world. Paul describes Him:

Who, being in very nature God, did not consider equality with God something to be grasped, but made himself nothing, taking the very nature of a servant, being made in human likeness. And being found in appearance as a man, he humbled himself and became obedient to death—even death on a cross! (Phil. 2:6-8).

For what purpose? 1 Pet. 3:18 says, *to bring you to God*. Not only did Christ's death pay our sin debt—it reconciled us to God. The day Jesus died was the day our life began.

PRAYER: *Father, I rejoice today that when Your Son died at Calvary the veil of the Temple "was rent in twain." Thank You for that wonderful day of atonement. I'm grateful that nothing stands between us. In Jesus' name I pray. Amen.*

THINK ABOUT THIS: He became like us so that we could become like Him.

—Stan Toler

GAL. 2:20

I have been crucified with Christ and I no longer live, but Christ lives in me. The life I live in the body, I live by faith in the Son of God, who loved me and gave himself for me.

People essentially live in one of three realms: the realm of sin, the realm of self, or the realm of the Spirit.

Those who live in the realm of sin are headed for a dead end, for *the wages of sin is death* (Rom. 6:23). The very nature of sin is fatal. It destroys people. It destroys relationships. It destroys finances. It destroys dreams and ambitions.

Those who live life only for self find life equally frustrating. The apostle Paul talks about how confusing his life was before he entered into the realm of life in the Spirit: *I do not understand what I do. For what I want to do I do not do, but what I hate I do* (Rom. 7:15). People who live selfishly are never satisfied.

On the other hand, life in the Spirit, the crucified life, brings fulfillment. Sin is put to death, self no longer lives, and Christ lives His victorious life through us! The crucified life is a sacrificial life but is one that's spiritually rewarding.

I like the story of the hen and the hog. One day they were watching a demonstration at the county courthouse. People were marching for world hunger. The hen was especially moved by the great cause. She looked to the hog and said, "You know, we ought to do our part to help put an end to world hunger!"

The hog replied, "You're absolutely right! What do you suggest we do?"

The hen quickly answered, "Well, if you'll give the ham, I'll give the eggs!"

Let me ask you—are you *whole-hog sold out* for Jesus? Or are you just donating an egg or two here and there? God wants to make something beautiful out of your life if you'll simply yield it to Him.

PRAYER: *I trust You, Lord, to take my life completely and make something beautiful out of it. I'm Yours completely! In Christ's wonderful name I pray. Amen.*

THINK ABOUT THIS: If you want an increase of Christ, there must be a decrease of self.

—Stan Toler

MATT. 16:24

Jesus said to his disciples,
"If anyone would come after me,
he must deny himself and take up his cross
and follow me."

There is more to the Cross than the death of Jesus, though that was a monumental, soul-saving incident. Jesus said that every Christian will have a Cross experience. *If anyone would come after me, he must deny himself and take up his cross* (Matt. 16:24).

What does it mean to bear a cross of our own?

First of all, it means that we must die to sin and self. When Jesus hung on the cross, He was bearing the sins of the world. We cannot die *for* sin—only Jesus could do that. But all of us must die *to* sin.

We must deny self. Paul taught the Galatian believers by his example to commit "self-icide." *I have been crucified with Christ and I no longer live, but Christ lives in me. The life I live in the body, I live by faith in the Son of God, who loved me and gave himself for me* (Gal. 2:20).

Second, bearing the cross means that we must die to the world. Jesus taught, *If the world hates you, keep in mind that it hated me first. If you belonged to the world, it would love you as its own. As it is, you do not belong to the world, but I have chosen you out of the world. That is why the world hates you* (John 15:18-19).

Must Jesus bear the cross alone,
And all the world go free?
No, there's a cross for everyone,
And there's a cross for me.
—Thomas Shepherd and others

PRAYER: *Lord, help me to take up* my *cross. And when the world hates me, remind me of Your unconditional love for me. In Your precious name I pray. Amen.*

THINK ABOUT THIS: Jesus died *for* sin that we might die *to* sin.

—Stan Toler

Day 28

1 Pet. 1:18-19

You know that it was not with perishable things such as silver and gold that you were redeemed from the empty way of life handed down to you from your forefather, but with the precious blood of Christ, a lamb without blemish or defect.

Calvary is the landmark of the Church. You can debate all the intricate details of God you want, but when it comes to the Crucifixion, you stand on holy ground.

An integral element of Calvary was the *precious blood of Christ* (1 Pet. 1:18). Who else has equaled this blood sacrifice? Many have claimed His name and trespassed on His promises, but no one has duplicated His sacrifice.

"Precious" is the word Peter uses, meaning "highly valuable, very costly, highly cherished" (*Webster's II New Riverside University Dictionary* [New York: Houghton Mifflin Co., 1984], 925). "Precious," then, is the highest word we can render of an act that changes the heart, renews hope, and transforms people and relationships.

It was indeed "very costly"—He gave His very life. It was "highly valuable"—touching every life that bid Him entrance to their hearts.

Those of us who know Him now as Lord and Savior

consider His blood highly cherished. It has become life to us.

PRAYER: *Father, Your precious blood is my life, and I am grateful. I honor Your name and claim You as Lord and Savior. In Jesus' name I pray. Amen.*

THINK ON THIS: When we think of the blood of Christ, we're prone to think of the gory side—violence and injustice. But what should capture our minds and hearts is that the blood of Christ represents a life—a life given for our salvation, our future, our eternal life.

—C. Neil Strait

Day 29

2 Cor. 5:17

If anyone is in Christ, he is a new creation; the old has gone, the new has come!

Comedian Jay Leno had a high school principal who didn't think speeding was a laughing matter. Leno committed his offense when he was a high school student and was suspended for three days after "burning rubber" in the school parking lot. The now popular talk show host has made amends by donating $250,000 worth of computer software to his school in exchange for having the black mark removed from his high school record.

The Lenten season is a reminder that all of us have the opportunity of a clean slate. We don't have to file any legal paperwork, do community service, or even make a large charitable donation. We simply apply the merits of the Cross. Jesus paid it all! Our sin payment has been stamped "PAID IN FULL" and signed in His precious blood.

Jesus paid it all;
All to Him I owe.
Sin had a left a crimson stain;
He washed it white as snow.

—Elvina M. Hall

We Protestants tend to take a different approach to the Lenten Season than our Roman Catholic brothers and sisters. I grew up in a predominantly Catholic neighborhood and remember how serious and solemn my Catholic friends were during Lent. I especially remember eating cheeseburgers while my buddies ate fish sticks each Friday of Lent.

Our tendency is to rush through this holy season without much solemn thought. We hurry to get to Easter. We focus on new clothes or new shoes and can't wait to sing the Easter songs.

Let me encourage you today to slow down. Take time to ponder the price Jesus paid for your salvation. Thank God for the new life you have through the Savior's atoning death. Think of what it cost Him for you to have a clean slate.

PRAYER: *Thank you, Jesus, that my record is clean. Help me not to hurry through this holy season. I want to have a greater appreciation for what You did at Calvary for me. In Your name I pray. Amen.*

THINK ABOUT THIS: Easter without a cross is a hoax.

—Stan Toler

Day 30

1 Cor. 1:18

For the message of the cross
is foolishness to those who are perishing,
but to us who are being saved
it is the power of God.

A third-grade teacher gave her class a "show and tell" assignment. Intending to teach the students about diversity, they were to bring something to class that represented their faith.

The first student stood before the class on "show and tell" day. "My name is Benjamin. I'm Jewish." He then held up a Star of David. The next little boy got up and said, "Hi! My name is Michael. I'm Catholic, and I've brought this crucifix."

The third student took his place at the front of the class. "Hi! My name is Johnny, and I belong to the Church of the Nazarene. This is a casserole."

While potluck dinners may have influenced our fellowship, the cross of Christ has shaped our faith. It is at the very core of everything we believe. It is the symbol of power and victory to every believer. But to nonbelievers the Cross is foolishness. They don't understand its significance.

Even the disciples struggled with it, some of them even seeing it as a symbol of defeat. But Jesus transformed it into a symbol of everlasting life! The apostle Paul spoke of that victory:

Having disarmed the powers and authorities,
he made a public spectacle of them,
triumphing over them by the cross (Col. 2:15).

Often we look at the sinful actions of worldly people and say, "They're sick!" But the truth is, sinners aren't sick. They're dead—dead in trespasses and sin. Dead people don't need healing power—they need resurrection power! The only way sinners can be made alive is through the awesome power of the Cross!

I'll live for Him who died for me.
How happy then my life shall be!
I'll live for Him who died for me,
My Savior and my God!

—Ralph E. Hudson

PRAYER: *Thank You, Jesus, for dying so that I might live. Help me today to share the message of the Cross with those who are perishing. In Your name I pray. Amen.*

THINK ABOUT THIS: The very reason Jesus died is so you could live—really live! So what are you waiting for?

—Stan Toler

Day 31

JER. 18:1-4

This is the word that came to Jeremiah from the LORD: "Go down to the potter's house, and there I will give you my message."
So I went down to the potter's house, and I saw him working at the wheel. But the pot he was shaping from the clay was marred in his hands; so the potter formed it into another pot, shaping it as seemed best to him.

Jeremiah's experience is a parable. It's the parable of God's patience and ability to take life that's marred and make it over again. How welcome such a parable is for those whose lives have come to failure, whose dreams have been dashed, or who are caught in the cycle of hopelessness.

The potter represents God, and the lesson of the parable is that God does not have just one plan. He is like the potter. His dreams and hope for us are often resurrected out of disappointments, failures, disobedience, and rebellion. But like the potter, He can take our lives into His hands and make us over again, shaping us as seems best to Him.

This parable makes two important points. First, we see God as the potter at the wheel, fashioning us, growing us, preparing us for life's journey. This is Creator God. He has made us from the beginning. He knows our ways, our talents, our frame—He knows all about us.

Second, when the form or life He has fashioned is marred in some way, the Master Potter does not discard it. He simply puts it back on the wheel and refashions it, restores it, salvages it.

This is the story of Calvary. It is about God taking life and touching it, changing it, restoring it. He has sent His only Son into the world to buy back the marred vessels, reshape them, and to restore them through redemptive love.

PRAYER: *Father, thank You for Your touch on my brokenness and Your patience with my waywardness. May I follow Your plans for my life each day. In Jesus' name I pray. Amen.*

THINK ON THIS: For the person who has lost hope there's a God who is the author of hope. His delight is to give it to those bankrupt of hope.

—C. Neil Strait

Day 32

1 JOHN 2:1-2

My dear children, I write this to you so that you will not sin. But if anybody does sin, we have one who speaks to the Father in our defense—Jesus Christ, the Righteous One. He is the atoning sacrifice for our sins, and not only for ours but also for the sins of the whole world.

John speaks clearly concerning sin and forgiveness. We don't have to sin. But if we do, we have an advocate in Christ, a heavenly lawyer who comes to our defense! Eph. 1:7-8 tells us, *In him we have redemption through his blood, the forgiveness of sins, in accordance with the riches of God's grace that he lavished on us with all wisdom and understanding.*

So the supply of God's grace is based on the provisions of the *offended one* (Christ), not of the offender. That's good news to a sinner! Further, God's grace to that offender is unlimited. Rom. 5:20-21 assures us, *Where sin increased, grace increased all the more, so that, just as sin reigned in death, so also grace might reign through righteousness to bring eternal life through Jesus Christ our Lord.*

Humanly speaking, we have limits to our grace, don't we? And often we measure our ability to forgive according to the "Three strikes—you're out!" principle. We even question, like the apostle Peter, "Lord, how many times shall I forgive my brother when he sins against me?"

We're scorekeepers.

Thankfully, God is not a heavenly umpire leaning over the balcony of heaven waiting to throw us out of the game of life on a called third strike. He is a merciful God. There's no limit to His grace.

His love has no limit;
His grace has no measure.
His power has no boundary known unto men.
For out of His infinite riches in Jesus,
He giveth, and giveth, and giveth again!

—Annie Johnson Flint

PRAYER: *Lord, I never want to be guilty of abusing Your grace. But it is so good to know that if I fall, You're there to pick me up. Thank You for being my Advocate. In Your name I pray. Amen.*

THINK ABOUT THIS: The church is a community of forgiven and forgiving former sinners.

—Stan Toler

Day 33

ROM. 6:23

*The gift of God is eternal life in
Christ Jesus our Lord.*

An old story tells of a wealthy father and his devoted son who shared a passion for art collecting. They had traveled widely to collect some of the most expensive art. When war engulfed the nation, the son went to battle. While saving another soldier, the son was killed.

On Christmas Day, the soldier whose life the son had saved brought a package to the father. It was a painting the soldier had done of the man's dead son. It featured the young man's face in striking detail. It became a treasured piece of art in the father's home.

When the father passed away, with no surviving family, the art collection was auctioned. On the day of the auction people came from distant places hoping to buy an outstanding piece of art.

The auction began with the painting of the man's son. But there were no takers. People grumbled—"Who cares about this painting? It's just a picture of his son. Let's get on with the good stuff." A man in the back of the room spoke. "Will you take $10? That's all I have. I knew the boy, so I'd like to have it." No one would go higher, so the man claimed the painting.

The auctioneer looked at the audience and stated that

the auction was over. Stunned silence filled the room. "Why?" some shouted. "What's going on here?" others asked. The auctioneer replied, "It's very simple. According to the will of the father, whoever takes the son gets it all."

This is a perfect picture of our choosing Jesus. When we choose Him, we get it all. When Jesus comes, He brings God with Him. We get joy, peace, righteousness, holiness, love, guidance, and protection, to name only a few. And at the end we have eternal life in His presence!

When we choose Jesus, we get all of heaven thrown in. God gives himself to us through His Son. Some tend to count what they give up to follow Jesus. The wise person chooses Jesus—and gets it all!

PRAYER: *Father, I am so blessed by Your gifts and so privileged to be Your child. May I treasure My inheritance in thankful ways. In Your name I pray. Amen.*

THINK ON THIS: When Jesus comes, He brings all the things of God and spreads them on the table of our hearts.

—C. Neil Strait

Day 34

2 Cor. 9:15

Thanks be to God for his indescribable gift!

What words do you use to describe redemption? God's love? Mercy and grace? Comfort and care? Words come up short.

It occurs to me that if God is doing the gift giving, it's impossible for us to describe its worth. With our best vocabulary, our words are still inadequate. Words just can't do justice to the works and gifts of God. Will we ever learn this? Probably not.

But God is more interested in our thanks, our commitment, and our obedience than He is in our descriptions. He needs neither, but He welcomes our thanks and praises, for He knows they do more for us than they do for Him. Some may think descriptions will get them by, but forget it. While He knows our praises will be adequate, our descriptions never will be.

Immediately preceding 2 Cor. 9:15, Paul thanked God for the Corinthian church *because of the surpassing grace God has given you* (v. 14). The word "surpassing" means literally to go beyond even what might be expected or what might be thought a possibility. The context here is Paul commending the church at Corinth for their unselfish love for fellow believers. It surpasses what was expected. It is then that Paul says, *Thanks be to God for his indescribable gift!* When it's God's gift, it's always surpassing our thoughts and doing more than we can adequately describe.

Calvary was God's gift to us. Indescribable? Yes. Understandable? No. Needed? Yes. And those of us who have accepted it echo Paul's thought: *Thanks be to God for his indescribable gift!*

PRAYER: *Lord, may I express my thanks for Your gift of salvation through my life, my obedience, and my love. In Your wonderful name I pray. Amen.*

THINK ON THIS: "Thank you" is appropriate but often inadequate when a great gift is received. With God's gifts, our best response is praise and obedience.

—C. Neil Strait

Day 35

LUKE 4:1-2

Jesus, full of the Holy Spirit, returned from the Jordan and was led by the Spirit in the desert, where for forty days he was tempted by the devil. He ate nothing during those days, and at the end of them he was hungry.

Fasting is a spiritual discipline that is especially meaningful during Lent. It is the practice of abstaining from food for spiritual purposes.

It has taken some time and maturity, but I'm learning the benefits of fasting. As a boy in high school, I would watch my Roman Catholic friends give up red meat on Fridays during Lent. I was challenged by their discipline so I started my own fast. I gave up things like broccoli, homework, and household chores! But as I've grown in my faith, I have fasted much more meaningfully, even for extended periods of time. Once I totally abstained from food for so long that licking postage stamps tasted pretty good!

Fasting has been practiced so rarely in the Church that we miss out on its blessing. I suppose we've been fearful that we couldn't live up to our Lord's expectations: *When you fast, do not look somber as the hypocrites do, for they disfigure their faces to show men they are fasting. I tell you the truth, they have received their reward in full. But when you fast, put oil on your head and wash your face, so that it will not be obvious to men that you are fasting, but only to your Father, who is un-*

seen; and your Father, who sees what is done in secret, will reward you (Matt. 6:16-18).

There are more ways to fast than just abstaining from food, however. Perhaps this Lenten season you might consider fasting from something else you enjoy—the newspaper, television, or the Internet. I challenge you to try it!

PRAYER: *Lord, this Lenten season, help me to give up some things that are important to me so that I might draw closer to You. In Your name I pray. Amen.*

THINK ABOUT THIS: Fast from selfishness, and feast on service.

—Stan Toler

Day 36

1 John 1:8-9

If we claim to be without sin, we deceive ourselves and the truth is not in us. If we confess our sins, he is faithful and just and will forgive us our sins and purify us from all unrighteousness.

Jimmy and his twin sister, Jenny, went to their grandparents' farm to spend the summer. Coming from the city, Jimmy and Jenny discovered a whole new world. They enjoyed spending time with their grandparents as they did their chores.

Grandpa helped Jimmy make a slingshot. Now, Jimmy couldn't hit the side of his grandparents' barn with it, but he practiced on anything that looked like a target. One day he was practicing by the pond in front of the farm house when he saw one of Grandma's mallard ducks swim by. He thought, *I'll never hit it.* But, nonetheless, he loaded up his slingshot, stretched back the band, and let 'er rip. You guessed it! Jimmy hit the little mallard in the back of the neck and sent it to duck heaven.

Jenny just happened to be watching, and like any compassionate sister, she immediately said, "You're in big trouble! Wait 'til I tell Grandma!"

Jimmy begged, "Please don't tell Grandma. I'll do anything. Just don't tell her. Please!"

They went in for lunch. After lunch, Grandma said, "Jenny, why don't you give me a hand with the dishes?"

Jenny said, "You know, Grandma, I think Jimmy wants to do the dishes." Jimmy began to shake his head back and forth. Then Jenny leaned over to him and whispered, "Remember the duck?"

The next day Grandpa said, "Let's go fishing!"

Grandma replied, "Why don't you and Jimmy go on? I need Jenny to help me get the laundry off the line."

Jenny responded, "You know, Grandma, I think Jimmy would rather stay and help you. Wouldn't you, Jimmy?" Then she whispered to him, "Remember the duck?"

For nearly two weeks, Jenny held her twin brother in bondage to his offense. Finally, not able to live with the guilt, Jimmy confessed, "Grandma, I killed your duck."

Grandma replied, "I know you did, Jimmy. I was looking out the front window when it happened. And the moment it happened, I forgave you. I just wondered how long you were going to let your sister make you a slave to what you did."

PRAYER: *Father, help me to be quick to confess the wrongs in my life. Thank You for Your faithful forgiveness. In Jesus' name I pray. Amen.*

THINK ABOUT THIS: Confession is a good stress reliever.

—Stan Toler

Day 37

2 Cor. 5:17

*If anyone is in Christ,
he is a new creation; the
old has gone, the new has come!*

At age 15 Phil Cookes was arrested for theft in a Los Angeles church parking lot. For 20 years he spent time between prison and drug addition.

At age 51 Phil Cookes became pastor of the very church he had robbed as a teenager. He said that "What the psychologists, psychiatrists, and criminologists couldn't do, Christ did" (*World Magazine,* 15 April 2000, 12).

This is Calvary in living color. Jesus restores, creates new life, changes things, does the impossible. What no one else could do, Jesus did. It's the story of millions who have experienced His changing, redeeming grace.

Jesus does not walk across the stage of life as the change agent, par excellent, to impress people. He did not stage Calvary to win applause. He did it to bring light to darkness and hope to despair. He does not do the impossible just to lead the pack. He did it to change things, to make them better, to bring God to intervene in misery and brokenness.

You can debate Jesus and His changing love all you want. You can marshal your research and align your facts in impressive ways. But when a man like Phil Cookes shares his life change through an encounter with Jesus Christ, all the debates and arguments are mute. Truth settles the case.

In a world desperate for authentic trust, standing knee-deep in broken promises, Paul's testimony rings with appeal: *If anyone is in Christ, he is a new creation; the old has gone, the new has come* (2 Cor. 5:17).

Billions of dollars are spent each year by people trying to get rid of old addictions, habits, scars, and bruises. What the billions cannot buy, Jesus provides as a gift! His promise is *a new creation; the old has gone, the new has come!*

PRAYER: *Lord Jesus, keep my heart and life firmly planted in You so my life will reap newness, growth, and love. In Your name I pray. Amen.*

THINK ON THIS: The only proof of God is what He does. He leaves convincing tracks in the hearts of people.

—C. Neil Strait

Day 38

JOHN 3:16-17

For God so loved the world that he gave his one and only Son, that whoever believes in him shall not perish but have eternal life. For God did not send his Son into the world to condemn the world, but to save the world through him.

Why would Jesus leave His throne in glory to come to this wretched old world of ours? And why did God the Father send Him in the first place? What was the motivation?

It was love. *For God so loved the world.*

O love of God, how rich and pure!
How measureless and strong!
It shall forevermore endure—
The saints' and angels' song!
—Frederick M. Lehman

It was love that brought Jesus into this world. That's why He left the riches of heaven for the poverty of earth. *You know the grace of our Lord Jesus Christ, that though he was rich, yet for your sakes he became poor, so that you through his poverty might become rich* (2 Cor. 8:9). Now, I know plenty of poor people who want to be rich, but I've never met a rich man who wanted to be poor.

Love was His motive for coming to earth, but what was His mission? Did He come to condemn us? To bury us in a sea of impossible commandments or principles? Not according to John's Gospel: *For God did not send his Son into the world to condemn the world, but to save the world through him* (John 3:17).

His mission was to save us, to draw us in, not to keep us out. In Luke 19:10 Jesus said, *The Son of Man came to seek and to save what was lost.*

PRAYER: *Thank You, Jesus, for the hope of eternal life. I praise You for giving up Your throne in glory for an old rugged cross. In Your matchless name I pray. Amen.*

THINK ABOUT THIS: Not only did Jesus die for the world—He died for *you*!

—Stan Toler

Day 39

EPH. 1:7-8

*In him we have redemption through his blood,
the forgiveness of sin, in accordance
with the riches of God's grace that
he lavished on us with all wisdom
and understanding.*

EPH. 2:10

*We are God's workmanship, created in
Christ Jesus to do good works, which
God prepared in advance for us to do.*

Donatello was laboring at a piece of marble intending to sculpt a famous person when a flaw appeared. He discarded the stone. From that discarded stone Michelangelo carved his famous statue of David.

This is a reminder that God has come to the ash heap of humanity to pick up the discarded lives and mold them into something beautiful for His glory. It is the story of redemption—the story of God sending His Son to our rescue, to find us and make us anew.

Salvation comes from the word "salvage." It means to rescue something thrown away, badly disfigured, or rejected. Redemption means all of this for us. Sin had placed us in a spiritual junkyard. But Jesus came and at Calvary bought us back for God's use.

Isaiah, an Old Testament prophet, discovered this workmanship of the Creator. In the Temple, in a moment of worship, he saw his plight and prayed, *Woe to me! . . . I am ruined! For I am a man of unclean lips, and I live among a people of unclean lips, and my eyes have seen the King, the LORD Almighty.* He explains what happened next: *Then one of the seraphs flew to me with a live coal in his hand, which he had taken with tongs from the altar. With it he touched my mouth and said, "See, this has touched your lips; your guilt is taken away and your sin atoned for." Then I heard the voice of the Lord saying, "Whom shall I send? And who will go for us?" And I said, "Here am I. Send me!"* (Isa. 6:5-8).

We are forever running into God's work in the lives of people—people who were broken but sculptured by God's grace and power. If we learn nothing more at Calvary, let us know that God has the last word about our future. Each of us has opportunity to be fashioned by the Redeemer, whose touch and love bring newness.

PRAYER: *Father, in my moments of doubt when Satan tries to diminish my importance, remind me that I am redeemed and am a child of God. In Your Son's name I pray. Amen.*

THINK ON THIS: Too many go through life feeling discarded, unwanted, friendless. They need Jesus to see redemptive possibilities.

—C. Neil Strait

ROM. 6:23

The gift of God is eternal life in Christ Jesus our Lord.

If you could choose one gift, what would it be? A car? Clothes? Wealth? A house? A dream vacation? How could you choose just one?

Let's ask the question this way: What gift would you want that would last a lifetime? That narrows the choices, doesn't it? Try eternal life.

You see, all other gifts will be nothing at some point. Cars wear out. Clothing styles change. Wealth is soon spent, and houses decay.

Calvary is about eternity. Tomorrow. Next year. Many see eternal life as something they won't need for a while. Wrong. Eternal life is a gift that gives all the way to the end—and endlessly beyond.

Eternal life is a relationship with Jesus Christ. He is Lord, with all the benefits that such a relationship brings. When He becomes Lord, He brings God to us—God's love, grace, mercy, care, wisdom, protection, to name a few.

Eternal life brings wisdom and direction to all of life. To be related to God is to have His wisdom. To have His wisdom is to have purpose and direction. Os Guinness in his book *Time for Truth* reminds us that "Truth, like meaning as a whole, is not for us to create but for us to discover" ([Grand Rapids: Baker Books, 2000], 74).

Our chances of discovering truth are much better if we're related to the One who said, *I am the way and the truth and the life* (John 14:6). That's the message of Calvary.

So if you're choosing one gift, what would it be?

PRAYER: *O, Lord, amid all the choices, may I make the one that will influence all others—the choice of You as Lord and Master of my life. In Your name I pray. Amen.*

THINK ON THIS: Some choices have bitter, lifelong consequences. Choosing Christ has positive, life-giving consequences —and eternal life!

—C. Neil Strait

Day 41

Col. 2:13-14

When you were dead in your sins and in the uncircumcision of your sinful nature, God made you alive with Christ. He forgave us all our sins, having canceled the written code, with its regulations, that was against us and that stood opposed to us; he took it away, nailing it to the cross.

He forgave us all our sins. Seems impossible. Did He know how many there were? Did He know how terrible they were? Can God's grace and mercy be that forgiving? Yes, yes, and yes.

Joel's prophecy *He is gracious and compassionate* (2:13) is a good word for our waywardness more than 2,000 years ago. Paul later confirms it in his letter to the Colossians.

To be such sinners and then, because of Calvary, to be blessed by grace, mercy, and compassion is almost too much to understand. Our only legitimate response is wonder, praise, and gratitude.

For those who stand in need of forgiveness, this is a good word, a hope-filled word, a liberating word. It unlocks the prison of guilt and shame, for, as Paul wrote, *He forgave us all our sins, having canceled the written code, with its regulations, that was against us and that stood opposed to us; he took it away, nailing it to the cross* (Col. 2:13-14).

Forgiveness, transformation, and acceptance are great themes of the gospel. They're naturally hard to understand, because they go against human nature. But then, they're easy to understand when you realize that it's God, in Christ, who is doing the forgiving, the transforming, the accepting.

Something happened at Calvary. We may not understand it all, but we can experience it all.

PRAYER: *Father, I confess my sins and believe in Your redemptive love. Thank You for forgiveness and new life. Strengthen me to live as a child of God. In Jesus' name I pray. Amen.*

THINK ON THIS: Forgiveness wipes the past clean and enables us to live above guilt, walking in the new life of redemptive love.

—C. Neil Strait

Day 42

2 Cor. 5:18-20

All this is from God, who reconciled us to himself through Christ and gave us the ministry of reconciliation; that God was reconciling the world to himself in Christ, not counting men's sins against them. And he has committed to us the message of reconciliation. We are therefore Christ's ambassadors, as though God were making his appeal through us. We implore you on Christ's behalf: Be reconciled to God.

"Reconcile" is an exciting gospel word. It rings with hope and raises our anticipation. In a nutshell, the Cross is history's reconciling moment—it is Jesus bringing God and humanity together.

In the Greek, "reconcile" means "to render something otherwise." And no one can do this like Jesus. He takes the blackness of sin and covers it with His shed blood, rendering a person a child of God. Thus, a person is "rendered something otherwise." Sinner to Christian. Darkness to light.

Max Lucado writes, "Reconciliation restitches the unraveled, reverses the rebellion, rekindles the cold passion (Max Lucado, *He Chose the Nails* [Nashville: Word Publishing, 2000], 64). It does just about everything life needs to have done. In a world that has come apart at the seams, reconciliation sounds like good medicine.

Reconciliation invites us to a new journey, a new relationship, a new tomorrow. Lucado further wrote that "Reconciliation touches the shoulder of the wayward and woos him homeward (64). Jesus is the inviter. By His death He has made a way back to God. He invites all of us to journey with Him, back to the Father.

PRAYER: *Almighty God, thank You for the message and reality of reconciliation. To know that You have made a way for me back to You fills my heart with love and thanksgiving. In Your Son's precious name I pray. Amen.*

THINK ON THIS: Reconciliation means that God has bridged the chasm of sin by the death of His Son. We have a way back to the Father.

—C. Neil Strait

Day 43

ROM. 3:21-25

Now a righteousness from God, apart from law, has been made known, to which the Law and the Prophets testify. This righteousness from God comes through faith in Jesus Christ to all who believe. There is no difference, for all have sinned and fall short of the glory of God, and are justified freely by his grace through the redemption that came by Christ Jesus. God presented him as a sacrifice of atonement, through faith in his blood.

Here is a summary of the gospel: All are sinners who can be justified by faith through Christ Jesus. You don't need a Ph.D. to understand it, but you need an open heart to receive it.

Within the small summary is a large story, that of wayward humanity struggling under the load of rebellion and sin. Humanity was trapped in its darkness and would *fall short of the glory of God*.

It would have ended there had it not been for God. As a matter of fact, *every* human story falls short without God. Paul tells us that God did something about this human predicament. Humanity is *justified freely by his grace through the redemption that came by Christ Jesus*.

God presented him as a sacrifice of atonement (Rom. 3:24-25).

Only through the one with grace to forgive on a cross where He would give His life could sinners be set free. Sin demanded a price and *God presented him* [Christ] *as a sacrifice of atonement* (Rom. 3:25). God met the demands of sin at every turn on our behalf. He took our place!

How do we respond to such a story? What is our part? Paul reminds us that *this righteousness from God comes through faith in Jesus Christ to all who believe* (Rom. 3:22). To believe on the Lord Jesus Christ is our part of the redemptive drama.

PRAYER: *Lord, strengthen my faith, that my belief in You will be deep and definite. May I prove my believing by my actions and life. In Christ's name I pray. Amen.*

THINK ON THIS: We are constant debtors to Christ, who took our sins and nailed them to the Cross. He does not demand repayment, but asks us to believe and to live for Him.

—C. Neil Strait

Day 44

Col. 1:13-14

He has rescued us from the dominion of darkness and brought us into the kingdom of the Son he loves, in whom we have redemption, the forgiveness of sins.

Calvary was for us—you and me. It was not an event staged by God to get attention. We were Calvary's purpose. *He has rescued us.*

Why you? Why me? Why any of us? *For all have sinned and fall short of the glory of God* (Rom. 3:23).

Sin had imprisoned us, separated us from God, blinded us to love, light, and hope. *He has rescued us* become great words of hope to us. For all who accept Him are *rescued . . . from the dominion of darkness and brought . . . into the kingdom of the Son he loves* (Col. 1:13).

Once we know the reality of such a transformation, a conversion, a born-again experience, we forever know the joy of being rescued. Darkness never seems worse than when viewed from the Kingdom. Sin never seems so hideous and tragic until it is viewed through Kingdom eyes.

A fine Parisian cello was part of the plunder the Nazi Army took on its move through France. After the war, a Canadian instrument dealer bought this cello, which had been ravaged and broken into pieces by abuse. He thought someone might use it for parts.

As the man learned the history of the instrument, he began to see it through the eyes of a redeemer. He took it to a master craftsman who restored the cello at a cost of $400. It was later valued to be worth $25,000.

The cello's story is our story. Damaged by sin, broken and hopeless, we were rescued! We were redeemed by the Christ of the Cross and restored to purpose and hope.

Why? Because God is a God of love, redemption, grace, and forgiveness, who came into our lives to rescue, to bring "beauty out of ashes," to bring us into His kingdom. It's the greatest story ever told!

PRAYER: *Father, thank You for rescuing me, for Your redemptive plan that makes life new and puts hope back into my tomorrows. In Jesus' name. Amen.*

THINK ON THIS: Redemption is God's rescue plan for a fallen world.

—C. Neil Strait

Day 45

MARK 16:2-7

Very early on the first day of the week, just after sunrise, they were on their way to the tomb and they asked each other, "Who will roll the stone away from the entrance of the tomb?" But when they looked up, they saw that the stone, which was very large, had been rolled away. As they entered the tomb, they saw a young man dressed in a white robe sitting on the right side, and they were alarmed. "Don't be alarmed," he said. "You are looking for Jesus the Nazarene, who was crucified. He has risen! He is not here. See the place where they laid him. But go, tell his disciples and Peter, 'He is going ahead of you into Galilee. There you will see him, just as he told you.'"

If you choose to debate the Resurrection, you'll have plenty of takers. Or you can ignore it—many have. But debating it or ignoring it will not change the reality of it: *He has risen!*

Frederick Buechner has a keen thought about the Resurrection:

> There really is no story about the Resurrection in the New Testament. Except in the most fragmentary way, it is not described at all. There is no poetry about it. Instead, it is simply proclaimed as a fact. Christ is risen! In fact, the very existence of the New Testament

itself proclaims it. Unless something very real indeed took place on that strange, confusing morning, there would be no New Testament, no church, no Christianity (Frederick Beuchner in "Reflections," *Christianity Today,* April 3, 2000, 72).

It's a fact my faith can leap to. Embrace. Welcome. We see it all around us. Kennon Callahan wrote, "Where is Christ? Christ lives and dies and is risen again and again among the human hurts and hopes of the people God has planted all around us" (Kennon Callahan, *Twelve Keys for Living* [San Francisco: Jossey Bass Publishers, 1998], 177).

PRAYER: *Father, thank You that every day I see Your grace and power being lived out in my world.*

THINK ON THIS: The Resurrection has its critics who have not proved their point. But every day, through the lives of believers, God validates the resurrected life of His Son.

—C. Neil Strait

Day 46

Luke 24:1-6

On the first day of the week, very early in the morning, the women took the spices they had prepared and went to the tomb. They found the stone rolled away from the tomb, but when they entered, they did not find the body of the Lord Jesus. While they were wondering about this, suddenly two men in clothes that gleamed like lightning stood beside them. In their fright the women bowed down with their faces to the ground, but the men said to them, "Why do you look for the living among the dead? He is not here; he has risen!"

He has risen! Three words of grand truth. How do they fit in with modern sophistication? They don't. How will they play among unbelievers? They may not. How do we explain them?

If you want a tidy story you can prove, then the Resurrection is not the story for you. Will the secular mind buy it? Probably not.

Only through faith in the One who said, *I am the resurrection and the life* (John 11:25) will it fit. Logical? No. Scientific? Maybe not. Workable? Yes.

When we bring trust and faith to the tomb, it does not

have to pass all the tests. But the one test it must pass is the test of the heart.

PRAYER: *Eternal God, may my faith embrace the resurrected Christ, and may its truth invade every fear and ignite hope in my heart. In Your Son's name I pray. Amen.*

THINK ON THIS: The Resurrection story has survived critics for nearly 2,000 years. Its truth and power will survive forever.

—C. Neil Strait

Day 47

MATT. 28:6

He is not here; he has risen,
just as he said.

He has risen! The great words of the Church and its faith. Confirmation. Assurance. Words every Christ-follower clings to. Words that confirm the hopes and comfort the fears of every Christian. Words we live by. Words we worship by.

A risen Savior! These words speak of triumph, victory, life, and hope. They challenge us to ventures of faith. They assure us that God's power and authority reign.

While those who do not know Him continue their doubts and ignore His ways, they're not better in their living. Without Resurrection authority at the center, life is not meant to work. It's against the grain of God's design. The best life has the resurrected Savior at its center, triumphing over darkness, doubt, and death.

He is risen! These words give courage to every Christian and challenge to every church. He is alive—today! Now! In our situation. He is walking among His people, along their loneliest roads and darkest nights, whispering in their ears, *Surely I am with you always, to the very end of the age* (Matt. 28:20).

I'm reminded of a little boy who had suffered serious injuries from an auto accident. As the nurses were prepping him for surgery, one of them noticed his unusual calm. She said, "You're a brave little boy—you don't seem scared at all." The boy replied, "My mommy's here, and she's going to surgery with me. She'll take care of me." How like the assurance of the Christian! A resurrected Savior is with us, He will be with us in life's worst, present with His authority and love, rolling back the fears and raising the banner of hope over our situations.

PRAYER: *Lord Jesus, I worship You as Savior and resurrected Lord. Teach me to walk each day in the confidence of Your care and guidance. In Your name I pray. Amen.*

THINK ON THIS: Only the Christian has authentic hope. All others must say, "I hope so."

—C. Neil Strait